To My Son with Love

Other books by

Susan Polis Schutz

Come Into the Mountains, Dear Friend
I Want to Laugh, I Want to Cry
Peace Flows from the Sky
Having a Baby Is a Beautiful Miracle of Love and Life
Yours If You Ask
Love, Live & Share
Find Happiness in Everything You Do
Take Charge of Your Body
by Susan Polis Schutz and Katherine F. Carson, M.D.
Don't Be Afraid to Love
To My Daughter with Love
on the Important Things in Life
Love Love Love

To My Son with Love

Susan Polis Schutz

Designed and Illustrated by
Stephen Schutz

Blue Mountain Press ®

Boulder, Colorado

Library of Congress Catalog Card Number: 88-70960
ISBN: 0-88396-268-3

▐ design on book cover is registered in the U.S. Patent and Trademark Office.

Manufactured in Singapore.

Blue Mountain Press ®

P.O. Box 4549, Boulder, Colorado 80306

CONTENTS

This book is lovingly dedicated to my two wonderful sons, Jorian Polis Schutz and Jared Polis Schutz, and to the rest of my beautiful family.

INTRODUCTION

I never thought that I wanted to be a mother. But when I had my first son, I discovered a new dimension in life—one that I never dreamed could be so fulfilling.

Being a mother, loving my husband and interacting with my family became more important to me than my career; in fact, they became the most important part of my life.

I then had a daughter and another son, and together with Stephen we became a cocoon of love. We worked together and played together, laughed and cried together, and grew side by side.

TO MY SON, WITH LOVE is written to my two sons—one who is on the path of growing up to be a man and one who is no longer a baby but just a little boy. I have written poems to my sons since they were born. This book reflects years of feelings and emotions towards them.

It is so amazing to watch your children grow. Every day has been a complete miracle filled with an enormous amount of love for them. And, as my sons continue to grow, I can only hope that the world will be peaceful and that they will be happy, successful, content and touched with a lot of love.

My sons
I want you to know
that wherever you go
or whatever you think
you can always depend
on me
for complete and absolute
understanding
support
and love
forever

Susan Polis Schutz

To My Wonderful Son

To see you happy
laughing and joking
smiling and content
striving towards goals of your own
accomplishing what you set out to do
having fun with yourself and your friends
capable of loving and being loved
is what I always wished for you

Today I thought about your handsome face
and felt your excitement for life
and your genuine happiness
and I, as your mother, burst with pride
as I realized that my dreams for you came true
What an extraordinary person you have become
and as you continue to grow
please remember always
how very much
I love you

I Enjoy You So Much, My Son

I feel so fortunate to have you
for a son
I love your bright face
when we talk seriously about the world
I love your smile
when you laugh at the inconsistencies
in the world
I love your eyes
when you are showing emotion
I love your mind
when you are discovering new ideas
for exploring
I love your ideas
when you are creating new concepts and
imaginary dreams
Many people tell me that
they cannot talk to their children
that they cannot wait for them
to leave home
I want you to know
that not only do I enjoy you
I look forward to any time we can
spend together
As you get older
not only will you always be my
adored son
but you will always be my dear friend
As your mother
I am so proud of you
and my love for you
just keeps getting stronger and stronger

My Son, You Can Always Depend on Me

Sometimes I talk to you
and I am not really sure
what you are thinking
It is so important
to let your feelings be known
Men were always taught
to hide their feelings and emotions
I want you to know that
this not only is wrong
it is harmful
Talk to someone
Write your feelings down
Create something based on your feelings
but do not keep them inside
Never be afraid to
be honest with people
And certainly never be afraid to
be honest with yourself
You are such an
interesting, sensitive
intelligent person
who has so much to share

I want you to know
that wherever you go
or whatever you think
you can always depend on me
for complete and absolute
understanding
support
and love
forever

To My Son, I Love You

It seems like just
a little while ago
you raised your tiny head
and smiled at me
for the first time
and I smiled back with tears
I loved you so much then
Though you are older now
living your dreams
pursuing your own goals
I still look at your beautiful smile
to know that things are all right with you
and I am so very proud of you
and I love you even more now

*Dreams can come true
if you take the time to
think about what you want in life . . .
Get to know yourself
Find out who you are
Choose your goals carefully
Be honest with yourself
But don't think about yourself so much
that you analyze every word and action
Don't become preoccupied with yourself
Find many interests and pursue them
Find out what is important to you
Find out what you are good at
Don't be afraid to make mistakes
Work hard to achieve successes
When things are not going right
don't give up—just try harder
Find courage inside of you to remain strong
Give yourself freedom to try out new things
Don't be so set in your ways that you can't grow
Always act in an ethical way
Laugh and have a good time
Form relationships with people you respect
Treat others as you want them to treat you
Be honest with people
Accept the truth
Speak the truth
Open yourself up to love
Don't be afraid to love
Remain close to your family
Take part in the beauty of nature
Be appreciative of all that you have
Help those less fortunate than you
Try to make other lives happy
Work towards peace in the world
Live life to the fullest*

*My son, dreams can come true
and I hope that all your dreams
become a reality
I love you*

Love is the strongest feeling known
an all-encompassing passion
an extreme strength
an overwhelming excitement

Love is trying not to hurt the other person
trying not to change the other person
trying not to dominate the other person
trying not to deceive the other person

Love is understanding each other
listening to each other
supporting each other
having fun with each other

Love is not an excuse to stop growing
not an excuse to stop making yourself better
not an excuse to lessen one's goals
not an excuse to take the other person for granted

Love is being completely honest with each other
finding dreams to share
working towards common goals
sharing responsibilities equally

Everyone in the world wants to love
Love is not a feeling to be taken lightly
Love is a feeling to be cherished
nurtured and cared for
Love is
the reason for life

Love is so important. I hope that you will experience a beautiful love forever with someone. This poem expresses a very small part of the love that Daddy and I feel for each other. There are not enough words to express all that love means to me. I know that you will discover your own meaning.

*M*any people
go from one thing
to another
searching for happiness
But with each
  new venture
they find themselves
more confused
and less happy
until they discover
that what they are
searching for
is inside themselves
and what will make them happy
is sharing their real selves
with the ones they love

*D*on't be afraid
to love someone
totally and completely
Love is the most fulfilling
and beautiful feeling
in the world
Don't be afraid that you will
get hurt
or that the other person
won't love you as much
There is a risk in
everything you do
and the rewards
are never as great
as what love can bring
So let yourself get involved
completely and honestly
and enjoy the possibility
that what happens
might be the only real
source of happiness

To My Son, with Love

A mother tries to provide her son
with insight into the important
things in life
in order to make his life
as happy and fulfilling as possible

A mother tries to teach her son
to be kind and generous towards other people
to be honest and forthright at all times
to be fair, treating men and women equally
to respect and learn from older people
to know himself very well
to understand his strong and weak points
to accept criticism and learn from his mistakes
to have many interests to pursue
to have many goals to follow
to work hard to reach these goals

A mother tries to teach her son
to have a strong set of values and beliefs
which he will always live by
and not be afraid to defend
to listen to his intelligence
to laugh and enjoy life
to appreciate the beauty of nature

A mother tries to teach her son
that being manly means being human
that he should express his feelings openly
   and honestly at all times
that he does not always have to be strong and stoic
that he should not be afraid to show his emotions

A mother tries to teach her son
to enter into a relationship with a woman
worthy on every level with himself
to listen to her, be gentle with her
to be completely truthful with her
to always respect her and treat her as he
    would want to be treated
to realize that love is the best emotion
    that anyone can have
to value the family unit as the basis of all stability

If I have provided you with an insight
into most of these things
then I have succeeded as a mother
in what I hoped to accomplish in raising you
If many of these things slipped by
while we were all so busy
I have a feeling that you know them anyway
However, I know I have emphasized to you
to be yourself at all times
to be proud and confident
to appreciate the value of love
I have loved you so deeply at all times
I have supported you at all times
I have always treated you as a person in
    charge of your own life
And as a proud mother, a person and as a friend
I will always continue to
love and support
everything you are
and everything you do
my beautiful son

My Son, I Love You

*As you keep growing and learning
striving and searching
it is very important
that you pursue your own interests
without anything holding you back
It will take time
to fully understand yourself
and to discover what you
want out of life
As you keep growing and learning
striving and searching
I know that the steps in your journey
will take you on the right path
Whatever happens in the future
I will always be rooting
for your happiness and success
and you can always depend
on my love and support*

I Hope that the Harshness of the World
Does Not Affect Your Sensitive Ways

When I think about you
I often wonder what
you will be doing
when you are older
I worry about the harshness of the world
affecting your sensitive ways
You are so kind
so generous
so good
so honest
I hope that you will always be
surrounded by all the
beautiful things in the world
As I watch
with extreme pride and happiness
every step that you take
towards manhood
I want you to know
that I will always
love you dearly

*M*en are told by society that
they always have to be strong
and put on a tough exterior
to block out all sensitive
"unmanly" feelings
It is drilled into men from birth
that they are leaders
that they must achieve
that they must succeed in a career
Men are judged their whole lives
by the power they have
and how much money they earn
What a terrible burden this must be

My son
the role society has imposed
on men and women is very damaging
All people should be free to
think and do whatever they want
and act the way they feel at all times
regardless of whether they are men or women
You should not feel pressure created by society
You should cry when you want to
You should laugh when you want to
You must be the person that you are
Other people should never tell you what to do

If you ever find yourself keeping things inside,
please know that you will feel so much better if
you discuss these things with someone. you will
find that if you have a problem, no matter
what it is, there will always be other people who
will understand, and you won't feel so alone.

I Am Happy to See Your Sensitive Side
Through Your Strong Exterior

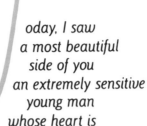

oday, I saw
a most beautiful
side of you
an extremely sensitive
young man
whose heart is
so full of love
I always knew that
you were this way
but you so rarely
show these emotions
You are developing into such a
strong, decisive person
but I hope you don't think
that you always have
to be this way
Your soft, sweet side
should be allowed to surface
more often
so other people can see
the entire you
My deepest wishes for you
have all come true
You are such an
outstanding person
whom I am so proud of
I love you always

My Son, Every Time I See Your Beautiful Smile, I Smile, Too

You are so stable
You don't want too much
You always seem to be happy
with whatever happens
I don't think I have
ever seen anyone so
content as you
You are so lucky to
be this way
my dear son
You will never be jealous
You will never be in turmoil
If only the world were like you
there would be peace forever
Every time I see your beautiful smile
I smile, too
and I relax a little
feeling so lucky
to be a part of your life
I will always love you
my dear son

am so happy
with the direction
that your life
is taking you
All of your decisions and
all of your actions
are so noble and intelligent
I often think about
how you were the same way
when you were a little boy
I hope that you remain so in control
of your life forever
And I want you to know that
sometimes you will make mistakes
and when those times occur
the proudest mother in the world
is always here
to encourage you
to understand you
to talk with you
to support you
and to love you forever

My son
I looked at a
friend of yours
and I thought about
how big he had gotten
and I thought about
how he was so much taller than you
However, I was very surprised
when I looked at you closer
and I could not believe what I saw
You are bigger than your friend
and several inches taller
I guess you are growing up
and I am hardly realizing it
because it seems
like such a short time ago
that you were playing with your
trucks and lizards
I hope that I am giving
you enough freedom
on your path to manhood
As you continue to grow
and with everything
that you do in life
always know
that my love and support
are with you always

ou are growing up
so fast
I look at you
with tears of happiness
sprinkled with some
tears of sadness
Sadness —
because you are no longer
my little baby
bobbling your cute
head up and down
But deep happiness —
because of the
new person you
are becoming
What an incredible feeling
to see my beautiful little boy
growing up to be a
beautiful man

A Dialogue with You When You Were Four Years Old

Sweet Angel
I was only joking when
I shook out the sand
in your shoes and said
"You brought the
whole sandbox home
with you"
You said so seriously
"Mommy, if you want
I won't play in the
sandbox anymore"
Angel—
I want you to
play in the sandbox
I want you to
play anywhere that you
want to
I want you to
have as much fun
as you can
The dirtier you look
the happier I am
because I know
that you are
having a good time
But the thought
that you would
give up playing in the sandbox
to make your mother happy
brought tears to my eyes

y son
looked at
me with
his large
blue eyes
and said, "Mommy,
please don't
finish your life story."
I asked him why.
He didn't want to
tell me.
Finally he put
his mouth to my ear
and whispered,
"If you
write about your life
it sounds as if
you are old."
I explained to him
that I am only writing
about when I
was twenty
until twenty-eight.
He said, "Well, okay,
but I still don't want
you to finish it."
"Why not, honey?"
"Well, if you do, you'll
be more famous

and the phone
will ring more
and it will even
ring all the time
on the weekends
and then you'll
have to talk
to everyone in
the streets
and we'll have
to go to all the cities
and you'll have to go
on all those TV shows
and everyone will
say, 'Oh, Susan'
and you'll have to talk
to everyone
and you will be
a big shot
and everyone will keep
talking to you."
I said, "Well, what's
wrong with all that?"
His eyes got
bigger and he
said softly,
"Well, then you won't
have time for me."

after I cleared away my tears, my answer to
you was "You want a mother who is not only very
happy with her family but who is also happy with
herself. My work as a writer is important
to me, but always remember this, nothing,
ABSOLUTELY NOTHING, is as important to Daddy
and me as you!"

Don't ever hurt
my angel
He's too sensitive
Don't ever lie
to my angel
He only knows what truth is
Don't ever be harsh with my angel
He is too delicate
Don't ever be unfair to my angel
He only knows goodness
Don't ever touch my angel
with maliciousness
If you do you'll have to
deal with
the devil
in me

*y little son
to walk
and play
with him
to talk
and listen to him
to understand
and comfort him
to love
and laugh with him
to teach
and learn from him
to watch him grow
and grow
and grow
as I grow and grow
beside him*

ittle one
you brighten up
everyone's life
that you come
in contact with
You go to sleep smiling
You wake up smiling
Your large eyes are so alive
with warmth and intelligence
Your dimples
are always laughing
What you say
with your cute baby accent
is so fresh and cheery
You understand so much more
than people think
Love and kindness radiate
from every part of you
You are love and kindness
Little one
you brighten up
my life all the time

$\mathcal{M}$y sensitive little son
who looks in the pond every day
in order to take out any bugs that
might be drowning
who cares about every living
person, animal and flower
as much as he cares about himself

My beautiful little son
whose eyes radiate all the
joy and goodness in his heart
who kisses my hand
and tells me how much he loves me
which is enough love
to carry me
through any day

Due to your extreme sensitivity,
I often feel a great need to protect you.
When you were 4 weeks old you
lifted up your head all by yourself and
you grinned at Daddy and me for
several minutes – so proud of your
accomplishment. You taught me,
at that early age, that you
need to do things yourself and
that I must not protect you from
all possible frustrations.

have been
preoccupied lately
Even though I have
discussed this with you
and you are aware
of what I am doing
it is hard for us both
When I think about all the time
I am not with you
I get mad at what is taking my time
I also feel guilty
I am sorry
that our precious time together
has been stolen
I know that
soon things will be back to normal
but in all the moments spent apart
please always know that I love you more
than anything in the world
my beautiful son

We have discussed with you and your
brother and sister the fact that Daddy and
I have a choice to spend a lot of time
fighting for what we know is right or to
just accept what we know is wrong.
We feel that we must stand up for
our rights and for the rights of others even
if most people say that we can't win
because we are battling an insurmountable
power. Daddy and I are proud of you
for helping us make this important decision.
However, we had no idea that it would
take up so much time and energy, and for
this I am very sorry.

ou have
made it so easy
for me to be a parent
I have always known
that I was extremely
fortunate to have
you for a son
But when I talk to
other parents
I realize even more
how lucky I am
I want to thank you
for being the fine
sensitive, beautiful
person that you are
and extra thanks
for being so easy to raise

I have always heard parents say
"wait until the terrible twos" or "wait
until the fearsome fours" or "wait until
the crazy teens." You never fit these
clichés. At every age you have been
so interesting and inquisitive, so
dignified and cute.
Every day and every year with
you has been a complete miracle.

My son
when you were a child
you were fun to play with
But now that you are older
I can do so many more
things with you
We can talk about world events
We can discuss life in general
We can make plans
We can read the same books
We can see the same movies
We can play sports against each other
Since we like the same things
we can enjoy so much together
I never thought that I could
love you more
than I did when you were little
But now that you are older
I have found
that I love you even more

*T*he love
of a family
is so
uplifting

The warmth
of a family
is so
comforting

The support
of a family
is so reassuring

The attitude
of a family
towards
each other
molds one's
attitude forever
towards the
world

If you ever find yourself chasing after the wrong things, remember this— the love between a family, and the moments spent together with your family and friends, are the only answer to all that is crazy in the world.

To My Son, I Love You

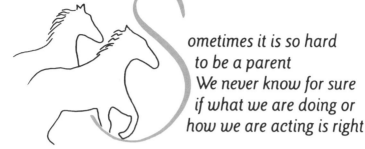

Sometimes it is so hard
to be a parent
We never know for sure
if what we are doing or
how we are acting is right

My son
sometimes it might seem
like I make a decision
that is not fair
I might not be
looking at the immediate results
but I am thinking
how it will affect you
and what you will learn from it
in the future

Since I consider you
a very smart person
capable of leading your own life
I very rarely
make decisions for you
But when I do
I want you to know that
I have a great amount of
sensitivity to who you are and
the foundation of any suggestions
I give to you
are made with
an enormous love and respect
for you
my son

What Is a Friend?

friend is someone who
is concerned
with everything you do

A friend is someone who is concerned
with everything you think

A friend is someone to call upon
during good times

A friend is someone to call upon
during bad times

A friend is someone who understands
whatever you do

A friend is someone who tells you the truth
about yourself

A friend is someone who knows
what you are going through at all times

A friend is someone who refuses to listen
to gossip about you

A friend is someone who supports you
at all times

A friend is someone who does not
compete with you

A friend is someone who is genuinely happy for you
when things go well

A friend is someone who tries to cheer you up
when things do not go well

A friend is an extension of yourself
without which you are not complete

We need to feel more
to understand others
We need to love more
to be loved back
We need to cry more
to cleanse ourselves
We need to laugh more
to enjoy ourselves

We need to establish the values of honesty and fairness
when interacting with people
We need to establish a strong ethical basis
as a way of life

We need to see more
other than our own little fantasies
We need to hear more
and listen to the needs of others
We need to give more
and take less
We need to share more
and own less
We need to realize the importance of the family
as a backbone to stability
We need to look more
and realize that we are not so different from one another

We need to create a world where
we can all peacefully live
the life we choose
We need to create a world where
we can trust each other

Though this poem was written before you were born, I feel that it still expresses my thoughts today. I hope that you will help to bring peace and fairness to the world.

49

Sometimes I worry
about you
even though I have no reason to
I worry about
when you are older
what you will become
whom you will be friends with
whom you will fall in love with
will you continue to be so creative
will you always be happy
and will the world be at peace
You have never given me cause to worry
It is just that I love you so much
and I hope that you
will be as happy
and peaceful
as you deserve
I want the best for you
in everything you do
Actually when I really
think seriously about the future
I think of what a wonderful son
you have been in the past
what a wonderful way
you have about you
and your extreme sensitivity
I am comforted
knowing that
because you are the way you are
the future is really quite predictable
and it will consist of
all the wishes
that I have always had for you
my wonderful son

*T*o see you smiling
To see you happy
To see you peaceful
is what makes me proud
As a mother watches
her son grow up
to be a young man
she can advise and guide him
she can offer her support and unconditional love
But she must give him
freedom to develop on his own
As I reflect on
your development over the years—
your strength of convictions
and your delight and excitement with life
I realize that
my wishes for you
have come true
And as you try out new things
and take new paths
while creating a life you want to lead
please remember that
I am always behind you
in everything you do
proud and happy
and full of love for you

My Son, I Am So Proud of You and I Love You

You are very unique and special
Your many talents give you varied paths to choose
Your phenomenal intelligence
always leads you to think so deeply about things
Your many interests
keep you constantly occupied
Your positive outlook
gives you the energy to
accomplish great things
Your determination
gives you the ability to succeed
in meeting your goals
Your excitement with whatever you do
causes you to always have fun
Your sense of humor
allows you to make mistakes and learn from them
Your confidence allows you to take risks
and not be afraid of failure
Your sensitivity lets you
understand and want to fight against
the injustices of the world

What an incredible young man
you are growing up to be
I was proud of you when you were born
I was proud of you when you were a young boy
Now, as I thank you
for continuing to grow in your own
unique, wonderful way
I am more proud of you
than ever before
and I love you

My Son

From the day you
were born
you were
so special
so smart
so sensitive
so good
It was so much fun
to watch you

As you grew
you became your
own person
with your own
ideas
and your own way
of doing things
It was so exciting
to watch you

As you grew more
you became more independent
still special
still smart
still sensitive
still good
I am so proud
of everything about you
and I want you to know
that I love
everything about you

Photo by Stephen Schutz   **Jared**

Jared

Jared
An individualist with
a love of knowledge and
a questioning of all facts
by his brilliant mind

Jared
An independent thinker
making all decisions on what he
knows is right
enthusiastically following his own path
regardless of what other people think
Extremely self-contained
never joining a crowd
Always busy with many interests
inventing new thoughts and games
with his enormous creativity and imagination

Jared
A gentleness towards people
a love for all animals
at home in nature
Barely noticing what other people are doing
but a deep understanding of world affairs and science
way beyond the most brilliant of minds
but limiting his interactions with peer groups

Jared
A good friend to his best friend
a very caring and dear son to us
easy to please
happiest with the smallest things

Jared
A genius
a dreamer
a unique child
of nature
and love

Photo by Stephen Schutz   Jorian

Jorian

Jorian
A love for everything
His absolute sweetness is
encased in a beautiful innocence
His laughing dimples
understand all subtle humor

Jorian
Always thankful for what he has
His easygoing manner
leaves him content and happy at all times
His light dancing eyes
show an intelligence way beyond his age

Jorian
His enthusiasm and concentration
His willingness to share everything he has
His absolute goodness
His complete gentleness and sensitivity towards people
make those he comes in contact with want to hug him

Jorian
His caring big eyes
so full of love for his family
His adorable, beautiful smile
lights up his whole personality

Jorian
An aura of peace and love radiates from him
An angel
A child of
kindness
sweetness
caring
and love

ABOUT THE AUTHORS

Susan began her writing career at the age of seven, producing a neighborhood newspaper for her friends in the small country town of Peekskill, New York, where she was raised. Upon entering her teen years, she began writing poetry as a means of understanding her feelings. For Susan, writing down what she was thinking and feeling brought clarity and understanding to her life, and today she heartily recommends this to everyone. She continued her writing as she attended and graduated from Rider College, where she majored in English and biology. She then entered a graduate program in physiology, while at the same time teaching elementary school in Harlem and contributing freelance articles to newspapers and magazines.

Stephen Schutz, a native New Yorker, spent his early years studying drawing and lettering as a student at the High School of Music and Art in New York City. He went on to attend M.I.T., where he received his undergraduate degree in physics. During this time, he continued to pursue his great interest in art by taking classes at the Boston Museum of Fine Art. He later entered Princeton University, where he earned his doctoral degree in theoretical physics.

It was in 1965, at a social event at Princeton, that Susan and Stephen met, and their love affair began. Together, they participated in peace movements and anti-war demonstrations to voice their strong feelings against war and destruction of any kind. They motorcycled around the farmlands of New Jersey and spent many hours outdoors with each other, enjoying their deep love and appreciation of nature. They daydreamed of how life should be.

Susan and Stephen were married in 1969 and moved to Colorado to begin life together in the mountains, where Susan did freelance writing at home and Stephen researched solar energy in a laboratory. On the weekends, they began experimenting with printing Susan's poems, surrounded by Stephen's art, on posters that they silk-screened in their basement. They loved being together so much that it did not take long for them to begin disliking the 9-to-5 weekday separation that had resulted from their pursuing different careers. They soon decided that their being together, not just on weekends but all of the time, was more important than anything else, so Stephen left his research position in the laboratory. They packed their pickup-truck camper with the silk-screened posters they had made, and they began a year of traveling together in the camper and selling their posters in towns and cities across the country. Their love of life and for one another, which they so warmly communicate, touched the public. People wanted more of Susan's deep thoughts on life, love, family, friendship, and nature presented with the distinctive, sensitive drawings by Stephen. And so, in 1972, in response to incredible public demand, their first book, COME INTO THE MOUNTAINS, DEAR FRIEND, was published, and history was made in the process. Today, after twenty years of marriage and spending all of their time together, Susan and Stephen continue to share their love with all of us.

TO MY SON, WITH LOVE is Susan's tenth book of poetry. It follows her recent bestseller TO MY DAUGHTER, WITH LOVE, ON THE IMPORTANT THINGS IN LIFE. Her other books include: COME INTO THE MOUNTAINS, DEAR FRIEND; I WANT TO LAUGH, I WANT TO CRY; PEACE FLOWS FROM THE SKY; SOMEONE ELSE TO LOVE; YOURS IF YOU ASK; LOVE, LIVE AND SHARE; FIND HAPPINESS IN EVERYTHING YOU DO; and DON'T BE AFRAID TO LOVE. In addition to her books, Susan's poems have been published on over 200 million greeting cards and have appeared in numerous national and international magazines and high school and college textbooks. She has edited books by other well-known authors and has coauthored a women's health book entitled TAKE CHARGE OF YOUR BODY. Susan continues to work on her autobiography and also writes music. She is currently recording her poems on cassettes to the accompaniment of contemplative background music.

In addition to designing and illustrating all of Susan's books, Stephen's art complements the words of many other well-known authors. He creates beautiful greeting cards and calendars, which feature his special airbrush and watercolor blends, his beautiful oil paintings, and his unique calligraphy. Stephen is an accomplished photographer and continues to study physics as a hobby. Together, he and Susan participate in many outdoor sports, such as hiking in the mountains, swimming in the ocean, and cross-country skiing along the Continental Divide.

Susan and Stephen have three children. They spend all of their time with their family, including their children in everything that they do. Half of their time is spent traveling, and the other half is spent working together in their studio in Colorado. Theirs is an atmosphere of joy, love, and spontaneous creativity as they continue to produce the words, the poems, the rhythm, and the art that have reached around the world, opening the hearts and enriching the lives of more than 500 million people in every country, in every language, in every culture. Truly, our world is a happier place because of this perfectly matched and beautifully blended couple, Susan Polis Schutz and Stephen Schutz.

Photo by Jared   Susan Polis Schutz and Stephen Schutz